WITH ALL FIVE SENSES

HANS W. COHN

With All Five Senses

POEMS

*Translated from the German
by Frederick G. Cohn*

MENARD PRESS
1999

Title of original text: *Mit allen fünf Sinnen*
(published in Hürth bei Köln in 1994
by Thomas B. Schumann, Edition Memoria)

Translation of poems © Frederick G. Cohn 1999
Other editorial matter © c/o Menard Press 1999

Thanks are due to the editors of
Oasis and *Modern Poetry in Translation*
where a few of the translations first appeared.

Cover design Charlotte Hodes

Worldwide distribution (except North America)
Central Books/Troika
99 Wallis Road, Hackney Wick, London E9 5LN
Telephone 0181 986 4854   *Fax* 0181 533 5821

Distribution in North America
Small Press Distribution Inc.
1341 Seventh Street, Berkeley, CA 94710, USA

ISBN 1 874320 21 7

Menard Press
8 The Oaks, Woodside Avenue
London N12 8AR, UK
Telephone and fax 0181 446 5571

Typeset by Antony Gray
Printed and bound in Great Britain by
Alden Press, Oxford

Contents

Publisher's Preface

Hans W. Cohn was born in Breslau in 1916. He left Germany as an eighteen-year-old to study medicine in Prague. Even then he was planning to become a psychotherapist, but decided that a medical background would be useful. The Nazi occupation of Czechoslovakia brought his studies to a sudden end. He and the other members of his immediate family escaped by the skin of their teeth and managed miraculously to reach England.

Needless to say, it was not possible for him to continue his medical studies. He became a bookseller, joined a community based on psychotherapeutic ideas, gained an honours degree at the University of London, and started his training as a psycho-therapist.

In 1960 he began practising psychotherapy with individuals and groups. A few years later his thesis on the psychological aspects of the work of the German-Jewish poet Else Lasker-Schüler was accepted for a PhD and later published by Cambridge University Press.

Hans W. Cohn has always been particularly interested in the philosophical dimension of psychotherapy, and was funda-mentally influenced by the ideas of Ludwig Binswanger and Medard Boss. He has written a number of papers on the phenomenological and existential aspects of psychotherapy, which have been published in professional journals. Most recently his introduction to existential psychotherapy, *Existential Thought and Therapeutic Practice: an Introduction to Existential Psychotherapy,* was brought out by Sage (1997).

The present book is a complete translation of the poems collected in the book *Mit allen fünf Sinnen,* which was published by the German publisher Thomas B. Schumann at Edition Memoria in 1994. Written in the seventies, they are Hans W. Cohn's last poems.

A leading German magazine, *Neue Deutsche Hefte,* said of Cohn's first collection, published in 1964 when he was already forty-eight: 'Hans W. Cohn is the flesh-and-blood manifestation of a European heritage going back more than two thousand years. The combination of traditional spirituality with penetrating analysis and an almost visionary imagination produces completely untraditional forms. It is astonishing that the work of this important lyric poet has not been published before now.'

Foreword by Michael Hamburger

It would be out of character – both his and mine – if I were to begin with regrets that Hans W. Cohn withdrew from the poetry scene after one book published in England and another published in Germany, apart from a few periodical publications. Since his English doctoral thesis on the work of Else Lasker-Schüler (published in 1974), he has devoted himself to his activities as a psychotherapist. A third collection appeared very belatedly, when the author had renounced all literary ambition. His latest book publication is not a literary work, but a contribution to psychotherapy and philosophy, *Existential Thought and Therapeutic Practice* (1997).

The fact that even his published poems are no longer noticed or mentioned is partly due to the nature of any literary scene, its exits and entrances, partly to the poet's retiring nature: he never sought to be praised or pitied as a victim of persecution or expulsion. Because in later years our personal contacts, which must have begun in the late 1940s, became few and far between, I can only assume that he stopped writing poems when he ceased to submit his later ones for publication. Cohn's earliest letters to me are undated, but they must date from before the publication in London of his book *Poems* (1950). This first book was already notable for its brevity and concision. It contained only seventeen poems, a severe selection from among many more, some of which I had seen in typescript.

From the start, I had found his poems appealing and convincing as very few others I had read in German of that period. This was also the experience of readers and critics like the poets Erich Fried, an early advocate of Hans W. Cohn, and Walter Höllerer. Christopher Middleton and I also included some of his poems (translated by Middleton) in our bilingual anthology, *Modern German Poetry 1910–1960* (1962), and I included others (translated by myself) in my later anthology, *German Poetry 1910–75* (1977). The present volume will, one hopes, bring him to the attention of more English-language readers.

In a short notice of Cohn's *Poems* (1964) in *The Times Literary Supplement,* I wrote:

> The most remarkable poems in this collection . . . are existential parables written with an extraordinary precision, and without the aid of rhetoric or conventional pathos. If they are all the more poignant for that it is because they have been refined and distilled to their essence, like certain short prose-parables by Kafka. The whole volume, in fact, is the work of a poet who confines himself to what is strictly necessary. Though it includes short lyrics in regular metre, others in free verse, and a longer poem in variation form, it is distinguished throughout by a scrupulous spareness, and the sensibility that has shaped the most memorable poems in this book is very much of our time.

In February 1974, Hans W. Cohn sent me his later poems. These were not collected until his 1994 German collection of which the present volume is a translation, but I translated some of the poems from the transcript for my bilingual anthology. Our meetings and correspondence became increasingly infrequent after 1976 when I moved out of London and Hans W. Cohn gave up literary work.

Though we were both pulling back from the bustle of the literary world, this silence between us made no difference to the old ties. From the first, his reserve and reticence had been part of the understanding between us, as when he had asked me not to include in my anthology a poem drawn from a particularly personal experience. Even his early poems had concentrated on what is existentially and psychologically general. It was to this that Hans W. Cohn confined himself, rather than the circumstances of his own sufferings and early struggles, of which I knew a little. All his short poems were reductions of experience to its bare bones.

In 1963, the journal *Neue Deutsche Hefte* first published the short poem:

> Two mirrors sit
> opposite each other
> and look at each other.
> Then they get up
> and go their own way.
> And both are thinking:
> how good it is
> to be in touch
> with someone.

This is a many-sided existential parable which incidentally anticipates the author's subsequent therapeutic activities, if one notes in it not only doubt and despair about contact with others, but also the need for seeing oneself in another and its therapeutic value.

Since he concentrated on the bare bones, the most essential and urgent of human needs, and had found a sphere in which he could share and ease other people's suffering, it was understandable that for him writing could no longer be of that essence. I too had long since come to think that even good writers are led by their profession (not to be confused with vocation) to write what is not of the essence, either for themselves or for their readers, which is why there is too much literature; and that when he or she has finally shed a little vanity, even for the author what matters is publication of the most essential work. If, for personal or external reasons, such work can no longer appear, silence is more dignified than routine performance.

Hans W. Cohn's later poems, too, are of that essential kind – essential for him and for others. For me, their publication means not only the fulfilment of a long-cherished wish, but an addition to the necessary and essential poetry of our time.

MICHAEL HAMBURGER

Michael Hamburger's edited and revised version of the foreword to the original German edition of this book (1994) has here been translated for Menard by Stephen Cang, apart from the quoted poem, which is translated by Frederick G. Cohn.

Frederick G. Cohn is the brother of the poet. He has worked in education and the social services and became a professional adviser in the Home Office, later in the Department of Health. Since his retirement in the 1980s he has written a trilogy narrating the progress of a young refugee from Nazi oppression. *Signals* was published in 1990, *A Lucid Interval* in 1999.

WITH ALL FIVE SENSES

The question

Having become
flesh in his flesh
the question digs
with a sharp spade
for the maimed
for the buried
answer.

Border crossing

1

When things could not go on
they decided to go on.
But they did not get far.

2

With his face to the wall
the father
with her face to the wall
the mother
with his face to the wall
the older son
with his face to the wall
the younger son

behind their backs
invisible boots
up and down

the father
with his face to the wall
invisible boots
the mother
with her face to the wall
up and down
the older son
up and down
the younger son
invisible boots

behind their backs
up and down
with their faces to the wall.

3

There is a game
called: border crossing.

Try to imagine:
somebody puts you on his border
and tells you: run run
here is no place for you

and imagine:
you run
to the other one's border
and he tells you: run run
here is no place for you
and you run
back
to the border of the first
and he tells you: run run
here is no place for you

and you run . . .

the duration of the game
depends on
how clever you are
how plucky
how persistent
and how old.

Between border and border
there is no man's land
here you can sit down
and undisturbed
perish.

Even now Poland

Sometimes it seems
as if he had
never left Poland.

The thirst for instance
is almost the same
unquenchable
for there is no real
water.

He also finds himself
again and again
suddenly
in prisons
without credentials

or strays
through a flat landscape
between burnt-down houses
(only the chimneys point upward)
and abandoned rails

stares
at countless
crossroads
trapped.

Often he scents
as then
the oppressive smell

of dead horses
which cover the fields
with swollen bodies
carrying nothing.

Even now
when the enemy comes close
he creeps
into the next ditch
pulls the coat
over his head
and clings
to the warm fleece
of sleep.

With all five senses

1

Give the eyes
a lead:
quick is the tongue and blind
and damaged the road.

Risky enough
is the quest of the look
if it takes fright
the chariot of love collapses.

2

But what happens
to the skin
left
under the protecting cloth
touched by nothing else
but itself?

3

Sometimes
before falling asleep
suddenly
the taste of a different bread
from childhood
crisp and sweet

or even earthier
indescribable
a taste of a country
behind sleep.

4

The nose
for a long time deafened
in a world
of fragrant signs.

5

Nothing more open
than the opened ear.

To listen with one's eyes
to eavesdrop with one's tongue
to hear with one's hands.

To learn once again
to listen with one's nose.

With all five senses
to obey the calls:
belonging.

Father

Unlucky Joseph
who never escaped the pit
into which the brothers threw you

tireless tailor
of many-coloured coats
none of which fitted

lost in the streets
of your misinterpreted dreams
without ever asking the way –

only sometimes
when mending the shoes
of your sons
you succeeded at last
in making something real
rough
and tangible.

Mother

After her death
at last
the strong face broke
through the blurred mask.

Now perhaps
(if she could see it)
she would also accept the tree again
in front of the window.

No Peter

But he
is no Peter.

With clenched teeth
he casts his net.
He is weary
for he fished
the whole night
in vain.
The Master's suggestion
seems foolish to him.
He knows: here
are no fish.

He is no Peter
and his net stays empty.

Tale of an apostle

A chamberlain of the Queen of Ethiopia
a eunuch
drove through the desert and read the prophecy
of the dumb lamb led to the slaughter.

We know the tale, have also heard
how Philip the apostle
illuminated Isaiah's words.

The story goes they came to some still water
the eunuch said 'look there is water',
climbed off the wagon. Philip baptised him.

This, more or less, is the cheerful tale
of the chamberlain of the Queen of Ethiopia.

Other eunuchs travel through the desert
and maybe also read the prophet's words.
Apostles also come this way
and sometimes water brightens in the sand.

Yet from wagon to water the road
is very long
much longer than the span
of their castrated
lives.

Doubting Thomas
(A sculpture by Joachim Karsh)

The hands grasped
what cannot be grasped:
now they can talk to each other
and the left one knows
what the right one means.

The head
did not catch up
with the hands.
Grief still conceals
what they reveal:
He has no words
for their report.

The feet are silent
but they stand.

Praying disciple
(A sculpture by Joachim Karsh)

Not one of those
who could explain the message

he received it
and simply
folded his hands over it.

Also he cannot look at
what knocks under his fingers:
because he has sent off
his eyes
to the place
from where the message reached him
and is waiting patiently
for their return.

Does he know
what his crossed legs
affirm?

His mouth mirrors
suffering and stillness
the pulse in the lap of the hands.

The end of the sky

Each morning
he steps to the window
and sees the black cloud
gulp down the sky
into its swelling belly.

The end of the sky is close
he has worked out
the day and hour.

One morning
he sees the last piece of sky
disappear
in the swollen belly.

The end of the sky has come
he draws the curtains.
His calculation is correct.

There is still another window
and behind it
sky in abundance.
But he walled it up
a long time ago.

Doves and toads

There he squats
among the toads
that sprang from his lips.

He thought they were all doves
messengers of love
when he still cradled them on his tongue
in the nest of his mouth.

Hands

Two hands
twirl
a cork
with small
careful
turns
between thumb
and middlefingers.

The hands of a man
in his fifties
thin-skinned
already shrivelled.

Twirling the cork.

He is alarmed:
they are his own.

Enemy

When the lord of the fortress
sees from his lookout
the unarmed man
coming nearer
he shouts: enemy!
pulls up the bridge
and fires.

Birthday

This year
led him to the very brink
of the question.

If he did not wish to plunge down
he had at last
to turn
and face the answer
that stood behind him.

Fall

One morning
his face fell from the mirror
into his hands:

he let it fall.

Veterinary surgeon

Concerned
for other people's
cats and dogs

with tender fingers
eyes and ears
open to every sign of life
of the suffering creature

while in the cellar
his own hungry cats are yowling
his own beaten dogs dying.

Precaution

Look after
the vessels:
Make them leak-proof
solder the cracks.

A shallow plate
is of little use
in the uneasy hand.

It is hard
perhaps impossible
to pick up
the spilt love
from the tiles.

Rebellion of the body

At last the enslaved body rebelled
against him.

A whole life
shut off from water and light
chained to the dread of blow and fall

at last it rebelled and chased
the big-headed master
through the canals of fear

tore from his eyes the sleep
and held him into the icy winds
of wakefulness.

Mending nets

He sits in the corner
and mends his net.

With damaged nets
you cannot go fishing.

Sometimes he is disheartened
finds
always new holes.

Then again
his spirit rises
dreams of a perfect net.

In the meantime
the others go fishing.

The skin

But he
does not bring his skin to market
guards it carefully
against the clutches of the world.

Untouched
with every day it becomes
a little more precious
a little more vulnerable
a little paler

and shrinks
becomes gradually too tight
to jump out of.

Flooding

Next morning
sadness overflowed
the banks of the river.

It leant heavily
against the front door
he could not open it any more.

A little later
he saw once again through the window
the house of his neighbour.

But he could not find anything
not even a plank
to get across.

Expulsion

In the middle of the night
he got up
went to the stables
and drove out
overweight wishes.

He could not afford any longer
to fatten them.

Before going to sleep

Of course the children
fit in between themselves and sleep
another glass of milk
another story
will there be thunder?
the moon is too bright.

But the grown-ups:
are they grown up enough
to go to sleep?

Loss

Many years ago
you put him into the small room
you put him away
into the special room
that you visited only rarely.

For all those years
you thought you were certain
that he stood there.

Now and again
you went into the special room
to see whether he was still there.
There you saw him stand
(did you see him stand?)
and took the certainty
(was it certainty?)
into the other rooms
that he stood there.

Then came the time of need.

Suddenly you thought
that he could help you.
You went into the small
special room :
he was not there.
The room was empty.

It was the time of need.

Now you do not know any more
whether you really put him
into that room –
was there ever anybody
to put into a room?

Disappearance

One morning
he could not find himself any more.

He had mislaid
or perhaps lost himself.

It did not come unexpected:
for some time he had
with growing concern
noticed how each day he became
smaller and smaller.

He had worked it out
how he could perhaps prevent
the worst.

He had taught himself
to speak with a loud voice
so that he could hear himself
if the worst should happen.

He had pinned on himself
coloured ribbons
to keep an eye on himself
if the worst should happen.

For all that it has happened.

He looked
in drawers and books
and found no trace of himself.

He walked through all the rooms
and listened:
he could not hear himself any more.

Fear

One day
(he fears)
the unwritten
love poems
will return
from their cold exile:
lethal arrows
of ice.

Therefore he keeps the windows
shut.

On mysticism

From the eightfold path
he has been barred
and has not been invited
to the spiritual wedding.

But yesterday he bought himself
a cornflower-blue
cup
and the ball of a child
sometimes makes a breach
in the wall.

About speech

1

To this they agree
that words
need undressing.

But one of them
enraptured plays with the dresses
leads a dance with blind costumes

while the other
perplexed by the nakedness of words
is startled.

2

Slide your hand
between the words:
pits
bottomless.

Without the mortar of silence
the sentences crumble.

3

The burial of the word
does not take place
(as to be expected)
in silence.

Obituaries rain
loudly and wordily.

Also it remains to be said
that lovers still do not
greet each other
with mathematical theorems.

And the children
still say
'mummy'
and 'my doll'
and 'come on'.

Morning

From the desk
the eye of the last blossom
on the exhausted tree.

The sky falls through the window
like a stone.

The limbs feel pain
after the beatings of dreams.

Dusty throat
from nocturnal travels.

Without meeting

In the living-rooms
in the underground
in auditoriums
looking at each other
without opening the eyes.

In bedrooms
in the car
in the park
embracing each other
without touching.

In dining-rooms
in coffee bars
at gatherings
speaking
without communicating.

Many voices
little hearing.
So many meeting-places
without meeting.

Experience of summer

1

A bird whistles holes into the winter
the eye is breathing again.

2

Every year
spring circles in a wider radius
around the ageing gaze.

Every year
more subdued the calls of trees
and the language of lovers
less translatable.

Not yet born
the other closer spring:
one's own.

3

Is the strained eye
still innocent enough
to look at the naked sky?

4

Under the blue sun
enter into the lament.

Autumn knocks
but not all fruits
welcome us.

Heavily walks the breath
in no man's land
behind the seasons.

Aeolian temple
(Kew Gardens)

Castle in the air
held by pillars
on a gentle hill
ringed by bluebells
giant beeches guard it.

The wind of course does not live here
it hangs around the river
where the boats are.

Sleep

Sleep: retreat
through dark passages

until suddenly
from the mirror of dreaming
you run into yourself

and wake colliding.

Sleepless

Foggy fear
in the ribcage

humming thoughts
on a lost trail

dream shreds
undeciphered

tapping sounds
of buried words

shattered night
sleep seeps out.

About him who stayed at home

But he is
the older brother
who does not squander money
does not take drugs
does not attend orgies

but stays at home
dutifully

and knows
that the love of the father
fattens a calf
in the stable:

it is not meant for him.

Wish

The sudden wish
to leave
the building site

the incomplete building
the pile of bricks
unused

to go away
and somewhere far
from the noise of the building
to check the blueprints
the plans.

But all is building site
and the plans
nobody has seen.

A question for Easter

Then it suddenly occurred to him
to compare his last poems
with earlier ones

and he discovered perturbed
that he had written
the same poems again.

Here and there they differed
in the punctuation
and also in the construction.

Nevertheless they were the same poems.

Then the question hit him:
how are new poems written?

A question for Easter.

Christmas

1

Again
on the way to Christmas
as ever.

Sometimes
the reflection of the star
on the brow of a question.

Also perhaps
an echo of shepherds' songs
from the nursery.

Now and again a book
written perhaps
by a distant relative
of those kings.

Who wants to deny
that somewhere round the corner
the child enters the world

Place and hour
to be sure cannot be worked out
and it is difficult
to arrive
at the right time.

2

It is not easy
to write a Christmas poem.

But a friend
related a few days ago
how as a boy
in the structure of atoms
in the dance of the particles
he felt the hint of inclining and drawing
                                        together
the mortar of the world.

Once (so he said) he stood in front of a wall
and felt with his eyes the pulse
of love in the stone.

Thus the account of the friend. Perhaps
a Christmas poem.

Easter

When spring
on his donkey
rides through the city gate
we throw our caps into the air
and salute him
as our king.

Later
when the hot hands of summer
bleed him to death
we stand aside
disappointed.

We had expected
different fruit.

New Year

It is easy
to throw away
the old year –
faded
the fruits consumed
those that were found to be edible
the soil used up
the pot cracked –
and purchase a new one.

More difficult it is
to replant
the old year
lovingly
in fresh soil
a new pot
so that perhaps
from the old
long suffering roots
a new one
grows:
more fertile.